The Relational Intelligence

The Relational Intelligence

The I.Q. of The Inter-Personal Intelligence

A Masterpiece in Personality Development

Ivan Pitzer de Souza

authorHOUSE®

AuthorHouse™
1663 Liberty Drive
Bloomington, IN 47403
www.authorhouse.com
Phone: 1-800-839-8640

Published by AuthorHouse   08/22/2012

ISBN: 978-1-4678-7306-2 (sc)
ISBN: 978-1-4678-7305-5 (hc)
ISBN: 978-1-4678-7304-8 (e)

Library of Congress Control Number: 2011961020

CONTENTS

FOREWORD

The focus of this book is on the concept of interrelationship as our duty, as suggested by the word *reciprocity*, defined as "helping one another."

Our mission is essential and founded on love and compassion within unrestricted human solidarity. My experience as a psychotherapist has always been very rewarding, and I have been honored to support the author of this book as wife and work companion, sharing the guidelines of each assessment and training given to those who were seeking our help. We have encouraged many who needed to understand their roles within the dynamics of their personalities and the framework of personal interrelationships.

The author goes beyond the superficial traits of a relationship to a closer assessment, evaluating motivations and frustrations as dynamic factors that begin with what a person wants to achieve for his—or herself and moves on to what can be expected from others in circles of friendship.

From our Master, we have learned the most important maxim of Christianity: "Love your God above all things, and your neighbor as yourself." Although it is a difficult mission, we must learn from Him that our solicitude will be a direct reasonable approach for a reciprocal kind of love.

Louraci de Moura Souza
Postgraduate in Vocational Counseling
Covington Theological Seminary
Pensacola, Florida

PREFACE

Writing about a complex subject in a way that enables the reader to understand is not easy; it requires wisdom and creativity. Dr. Pitzer De Souza, in his book *Relational Intelligence,* uses simple language, enhanced with great wisdom, to impart his message and whet the curiosity of the reader to go deeper into the subject.

The book presents case studies and interviews—conducted by the author in his career as a therapist—to convey the main differences between simple relationships and true interrelationships.

In this work, he invites the reader to reflect on the difficulties we encounter in our journey of life and offers key strategies for obtaining success in our jobs and families.

The text is full of dialogues to facilitate the reader's understanding. It is worth mentioning that society will benefit from the rise of the theory of relational intelligence, because it raises substantial and important questions and encourages a careful look at human holistic relationships.

I recommend this book for the reader to enjoy. It will certainly inspire reflections and new insights for all who seek personal growth and harmonious relationships.

Rosane H. de Sousa
Graduate in Education, Federal University in the State of Bahia (UFEBA)
MA in Community Education, State University, Rio Grande do Sul
Academic Director, College of Education, Salvador, Bahia, FACESA

ACKNOWLEDGMENTS

I gratefully acknowledge and express deep appreciation to the many wonderful people who have been an inspiration in my life and have made this project possible.

To my dear parents, Jonas and Anna, for teaching me how to build a relationship with love, respect, mutual trust, and courage—and for establishing faith in the Lord of Eternity, Jesus Christ, God the Father, the Holy Spirit, and the Holy Scriptures as a rule of our confessional practice.

To my beloved wife, Louraci—who has been a gift and companion in my family, professional, and pastoral relationships—for her unconditional support, understanding, affection, loyalty, and love.

To my unforgettable children, Ana Christina, Ivan Junior, Debora, Elaine, and Milton—precious jewels who were grown with love and selflessness and now bless others in their vocations, their ministries, and their community service in the Lord's cause.

To the beloved congregations of the churches I had the privilege of pastoring for the past fifty years, in times marked by the integrity and fidelity of brotherly love between brothers and sisters in spiritual unity, uniting us with ties of Christian love, fostering close cooperation, and inspiring us to rejoice in the Lord's work and celebrate the ideal of loving of the Lord and our neighbor as ourselves.

To my mentors, Jacques Lacan, Carl Rogers, and Francis A. Schaeffer, who instilled in me an understanding of the human being, without preconceptions or discrimination, seeking to help and restore those who needed understanding, and encouraging me through the decades of guesswork.

To my professors at the Department of Continuing Education, Harvard Medical School, and the Postgraduate Association, whose support allowed me to expand my vision of building relationships in the area of psychotherapy.

To my faculty members, Rosane, Antonete, Brasilena, Jussara, and Everaldo; administrative staffers Elaine, Mark, Albert; collaborators

Heldislene and Jonas; and all the dedicated people who helped with our community projects, enabling our participation in the educational work of our city of Salvador.

To my dear nieces, Monica and Natalia, for their efforts at translating this work from the original draft in order to create an English-language version.

To my Lord and Savior Jesus Christ, all honor and glory, who was, and is, and is to come, who lives and reigns, who is the master *par excellence* of relationships, teaching the way, the truth, and the life.

Can two walk together,
except they be agreed?—Amos 3:3

Chapter I

Relationships of all sorts involve a process of stimulus and response. People relate to one another in a positive or negative way, developing an understanding between themselves about family relationships, the environment, work, politics, education, health, religion—whatever the topic of conversation and interest. It's assumed that our degree of intelligence is a determining factor in whether we're successful or unsuccessful in these interrelationships.

Yet often, an individual's IQ does not directly correlate to relationship success. Smart people do dumb things when relating to others, often missing cues, misreading emotions, or being unaware of the way others are doing the same to them. What does it take to be intelligent in a relationship? The answer to that question is the *raison d'être* for this book.

In the early eighties, there was a revolution in the understanding of intelligence, with Howard Gardner of the Harvard University School of Education proposing a new vision of the IQ that focused not only on problem-solving, mathematical logic, and verbal language as ways to measure intelligence but on the "multiple intelligences" we use to solve multiple problems (Gardner, 1983).

Gardner defines seven types of intelligence:

1. *Logical-mathematical intelligence*, the ability to deal with numbers and calculations; typical of engineers, chemists, physicists.

2. *Linguistic intelligence*, the ability to communicate verbally or in writing; typical of writers, orators, poets, ministers, preachers, politicians.

3. *Musical intelligence*, the ability to compose music and communicate, both in playing instruments and singing; typical of conductors, instrumentalists, singers.

4. *Spatial intelligence*, the ability to visualize and understand space and objects in the

internal and external environment; typical of architects, decorators, designers.

5. *Kinesthetic intelligence*, the ability of to move the body with grace and physical coordination; typical of athletes, personal trainers, coaches, trainers, dancers.

6. *Interpersonal intelligence*, the ability to relate effectively with others, trying to understand the individuality of each person and the goals that may facilitate the interaction; typical of psychologists, educators, therapists.

7. *Intrapersonal intelligence*, the ability of an individual to know himself and be in tune with his own feelings in interpreting individual satisfaction.

This theory of multiple intelligences gave me the idea for a spectrum of IQ that would supersede the traditional Stanford-Binet intelligence scale and contribute to a new understanding that intelligence is multifaceted, both in personal and interpersonal communication.

A person can use his intelligence to understand himself and others, and to correlate his own ideas with those of others, creating a common ground. Working together intelligently, people can build a reciprocal understanding that aims to achieve realistic goals in a meaningful and constructive relationship.

Before we start looking at ways to improve our interrelationships, as we will throughout this book, I'd like to share some thoughts and research on emotional disturbances, intelligence, and communication that will deepen and enrich our thinking on this important and life-transforming topic.

The Importance of Interrelationship in Emotional Disturbances

For many decades, our understanding of depression came from the great French sociologist Emilie Durkheim, considered the father of modern sociology. In his 1895 book *The Rules of Sociological Method*, he drew attention to the syndrome of *anomie*—the absence of laws, principles, or values that, as a syndrome, weaken the conscience and relax discipline, moral values, ethical concepts, and respect for institutions.

Durkheim defended the notion that human beings are highly social; he believed a person's integrity could not be isolated from moral values and from respect for the principles that govern ethics. An individual's conscience dictated immutable values, and changing those should cause an emotional disturbance.

At the time, such disorders were treated as diseases requiring hospitalization. In Paris, patients were isolated at Sapêtrière, a charity hospital—until, in the second half of the nineteenth century, Jean Charcot, one of the best clinical and medical professors reaching fame in the field of psychiatry, released bounded patients from their chains and started a new treatment for hysteria with his patients, allowing interpersonal relationships and adopting the analysis technique through a hypnotic interaction (Charcot 1885).

Charcot's use of interaction as a major treatment for his patients awakened the curiosity of Sigmund Freud, who left Austria to come to France and learn how to facilitate psychological interaction with patients who were no longer considered crazy, but simply afflicted with emotional disorders that could be treated through an interactive analysis to find out what was going on in their subconscious. Freud later introduced psychoanalysis as an alternative treatment for his own patients, and that revolutionized the care of mental illness in the new century.

In 1973, while attending one of Jacques Lacan's conferences in Paris, I got a close-up look at this period in psychological history. Along with my colleague, Dr. Monica Veras, I had the opportunity to visit that same Sapêtrière hospital after being unexpectedly invited by the director of the psychiatric department. Both Dr. Veras and I had an incredible experience leaning about the old "madness quarter" where the patients were in total isolation, locked in chains; at that time, emotional illnesses could not yet be diagnosed as neuroses or psychoses. These people were removed from their homes and confined in isolation from family and society.

Fortunately, we had permission to check out another open ward in a separate area where Charcot's patients were placed in open rooms, in patios next to one another. Here, the patients were no longer chained. They could go out on the balcony and be escorted to a more relaxed environment. By using applied psychology to facilitate an interrelationship, separating the neurotics from the psychotics, and taking patients to a chapel where they were allowed to meet relatives and other community volunteers, Charcot created an interrelationship approach that, in time, would enable the rehabilitated patients to return to their families and society.

Assessment and Treatment of Depression

Without an interrelationship-based care assessment and proper classification of emotional illness, patients can fall into a state of existential depression so severe as to appear pathological, a melancholic state that is ever more difficult to treat. As drugs are administered, patients become more isolated and lose all social contact, with no intermediate assistance to make the treatment more effective and speed the patient's rehabilitation.

Psychological depression, classified as an emotional illness, has become increasingly common, spreading through all levels of society. It can have a wide variety of social and psychological causes—including aging, trauma, post-war losses, isolation, and existential disappointments—and many symptoms are not yet well-defined with descriptive terminology.

During my graduate studies at Harvard Medical School in the Department of Continuing Education, I was motivated to select a course called "Assessment and Treatment of Depression in Primary Care

Setting" (2008), which examined depressive disorders and the relationship of subclassifications to treatment access.

I came to believe that the following steps are essential to an interactive approach to dealing with depression.

1. *Treatment* should be oriented and planned, with prescription drugs specifically selected for each individual patient.

2. *The patient's history* should be reviewed and considered independently as part of the case.

3. *The case study* should interpreted as a preventive or corrective action before any selection of antidepressants.

4. *The risk of drug interactions* should necessitate a practical strategy to consider other drugs the patient may be using when prescribing an antidepressant.

5. *Monitoring of cases* should be ongoing so that patients who have not responded to antidepressant treatment can try an alternative treatment, either without medication or a

combination of medication, with intensive psychotherapy for moderate cases of patients who could not yet be considered curable.

6. *Cases of long psychiatric treatment* should involve constant reconsideration of traditional procedures and prescription drugs; electroconvulsive therapy may be appropriate in cases of severe depression that does not respond to other treatments.

7. *Interactive help from the family* should be encouraged—in most cases, it contributes to signs of improvement. Alternative medicine should be considered of great value when it involves the family's participation. If the patient improves, a domestic strategy should be developed so the patient is not separated from family but has a loving-care relationship and support for reintegration into society.

Relationship Therapy

Rehabilitation centers that practice interactive intervention have achieved great results. Predictions of success have proven true at, for example, the University of California San Francisco, where treatment involves an eclectic collaboration between experts in psychiatry, internal medicine, cell biology, pharmacology, genetics, neurology, biochemistry, physiology, and mental health.

In addition to interaction between departments, these programs also promote a supportive therapy relationship between patient and family, which aims to facilitate interrelationship and interactive recovery from loss, isolation, and loneliness. The patient can then be reintegrated into a social life. This new method is showing amazing results. Programs are being developed to integrate patients with their families, resulting in outpatient treatment instead of hospitalization.

This new therapy is patient-centered and oriented toward family members, who are trained in how to relate to the patient and taught methods of interaction that can lead to an interconnection with their family member, restoring confidence, self-esteem, and a feeling of acceptance as part of the family and society.

This progress is made through methods of interrelationship that may correlate with the different links—mutual trust, shared interests, a feeling of sympathy and empathy—by which two people can achieve mutual satisfaction. I'm excited to be able to present information on these methods of applied psychology and person-centered counseling, with the interactions entered into as part of a relationship, and correlations that can be evaluated and enhanced by the determination that the one who sets out to help others helps himself.

Correlations Between High IQ and Emotional Balance

Most research indicates that a higher rate of depression is found among people who are pressured by strong emotions and frustrations. According to the Psychiatric Research Center of the state of California, those with an average IQ are often better able to relate positively. Another study indicates that those with the best chances of avoiding depression are people who have better opportunities to relate positively, and that there is a correlation between the ability to control emotions appropriately by using logical reasoning and emotional balance in a relationship built through links of mutual understanding with family support, according to several reports from the World Council of Mental Health.

In the introduction to his book *Emotional Intelligence*, Daniel Goleman presents a notable quote from Aristotle's *Nicomachean Ethics*: "Anyone can become angry—that is easy. But to be angry with the right person, to the right degree, at the right time, for the right purpose, and in the right way—that is not easy."

This brings us to the Great Equation: $IQ + EQ = IR$. At this juncture of IQ (traditional intelligence) and EQ (emotional intelligence), I will draw a correlation coefficient of the IR (interrelationship) as a major factor assessment, in which an idea, a proposal, or a viewpoint of one person will complement that of the other person.

I have been researching this topic since Dr. Catherine Fosset, chairman of my thesis committee, recommended a study from the University of South Alabama, Mobile, entitled "Motivation, Emotion, and Frustration as Dynamic Factors in Human Behavior and its Relationship to a Learning Process" (1973).

The first dynamic factor discussed was *motivation*, which always facilitates the learning process. An organism responds to internal and external stimuli in such a way as to maintain its equilibrium. The term *drive reduction* refers to the way an organism in a physiologically unbalanced state will learn what activities restore balance and repeat those behaviors.

The second dynamic factor, *emotion*, can become a source of conflict depending on the temperament of the individual and the ability to relate to others, show concern for their problems, and communicate throughout the learning process.

As a basic paradigm, one must desire a rational and sound relationship, work with the other person to develop a logical understanding, and finally reach a mutual meeting point between what is taught and what is learned as an effective interrelationship.

The third dynamic factor, *frustration*, was observed as a failure to reach the level aspired to and surpass potential barriers. It depends on the commitment of the individual who want to overcome his difficulties and disentangle all ties and chains for a better personal relationship with a constructive learning purpose.

The question of interrelationship will always be bipartisan—that is, between the one who proposes to make an interconnection, relying on himself as the one who takes the initiative, and the other, who becomes the object of interaction, evaluating the emotions and frustrations as seen in the person with whom he intends to interact, not taking into account their personal differences.

If the result is just a good communication-level dialogue, the relationship is primarily positive. However, it would always be more effective and efficient if it were a deeper interrelationship in which the parties act with reciprocity—seeking to understand not only the proposals and reasons of the other but the real reasons for the questions, controlling emotions and circumventing frustrations, evaluating and then overcoming hindrances.

It is precisely at this turning point that we should see an interchange of mutual interests in order to achieve the same purpose—true interrelationship—in a constructive way, to produce learning on both sides, and to work together toward a mutual goal.

The Importance of Connections in Our Intelligence: The Synapse Factor

There is a general concept that matches numerical and verbal data on intelligence, based on a person's chronological age and degree of maturity, to the conceptual information and perspectives determined by how quickly the brain is able to capture information and interpret it consistently. Mensa and Sigma estimate that the intellectually supergifted represent 2 percent of the population, meaning they're smarter than the other 98 percent.

The Triple Nine Society estimates things differently, counting geniuses as a mere 0.1 percent of the population. They are smarter than the other 99.9 percent because they have a much greater number of neurons than the average person.

The number of neurons in the brain determines the speed of reasoning; in the case of super-endowed, that reasoning is quite fast. However, there is another factor—the number of connections, called *synapses*, between those neurons. The super-smart among us are endowed with a secondary and higher ability to multiply those connections.

The ability to learn and store large amounts of information leads some of these individuals to become extraordinarily creative, improvisatory, communicative, and social, while others become focused on their own introverted world. The truth contained in our DNA supports the thesis that an intelligent person can be distinguished from another intellectual by emotional barriers, as evidenced in the thesis of Daniel Goleman's *Emotional Intelligence.*

Howard Gardner's theory of multiple intelligences, mentioned earlier, associates particular abilities and preferences with different types of intelligences that match up to certain vocations and carriers. It appears that a correlation of theories of cognition requires yet another new paradigm.

Chapter II

Relational Intelligence: The New Paradigm

To these other concepts and correlations of intelligence and ability I would add an intelligence factor of interrelationships—call it *relational intelligence*. This would be an indicator of a person's ability to learn from others, starting from his or her own particular point of view and integrating varied thoughts and opinions to develop a more sophisticated understanding. Relational intelligence assumes a common denominator between two people, avoiding bias and preconceived ideas based on cultural or religious barriers.

Most people do not easily give themselves to a constructive relationship that facilitates interaction. They hang on to their own way of seeing the world and adjust only reluctantly to accommodate others. By studying those who quickly and intelligently establish interrelationships, we can define correlations that can be applied to a reciprocal understanding, raising a new intelligence concept and identifying techniques that can help us all.

Words, Echoes, Gestures, and Signs Throughout Time

The history of human communication is long and full of cultural nuances. Cavemen from the earliest ages of man's existence left symbols on their cave walls—depictions of fighting, of shouts during hunting accompanied by screams, and of rejoicing for a successful hunt that brought livelihood to the community.

Early civilizations, such as the ancient Egyptians, used pictures—hieroglyphs—to write messages. Documents of the Ancient Near East show scenes of Egyptian religious tradition recorded on a papyrus—the leaf of a plant of the Nile, preserved by a dehydration process and written upon with special inks. Ceremonies are depicted with gestures and symbols of liturgical worship and sacrifice of animals, expressed in the form penitent constriction.

Later, the Phoenicians wrote words and, according to findings from the Dead Sea and in other caves, the Hebrews translated into graphic shapes the sound of the Lord Jehovah communicating to them through Moses on Mount Sinai, beginning with the Ten Commandments. They wrote the words with consonants but no vowels because they dared not write or pronounce the name IAVEH as Jehovah.

Conversation only came to be known as a positive method of relationship between people through the Greek philosopher Socrates, who gave his disciples freedom to openly raise questions about ethics, politics, and self.

The Socratic ideal of "know thyself" was based on a recognition of what would later be known as intrapersonal intelligence, providing an important insight about communication: before I ask something (objectively), I should ask myself (subjectively), "Why I am concerned about this issue? If I were in the other person's situation, how would I solve the problem?" Without this internal dialogue, there can be no empathy.

Although his approach was regarded by the rulers of his time as a "universal philosophy," it had the effect of encouraging people to have more positive communication by creating an ideal to be understood and practiced. In the Socratic dialogue, no person could be "the master of truth." Participation involving open communication would be interactive and bilateral, and only rise to the level of dialogue if the interlocutors came to a common denominator.

The Common Denominator: Our Conscience

Perhaps one thing we can all understand is how our heads can become cluttered with information, and how an inability to control our thoughts can affect our communication with others. Understanding the way we all struggle with memories, emotions, and intentions, fighting to get them under control, may suggest a common denominator that allows for flexibility and forgiveness in interrelationships.

Think of the brain as a crowded wardrobe. We usually place on the safest, topmost shelf a number of things considered very important to our sense of self-worth. We choose a numerical quantity of what we think we have, the sum of our own acquired knowledge and experiences, personal views, convictions, and recollections, and place them on the top shelves of our secret closets; we can open the doors to find out what we have saved or stored for our personal use, and access these things whenever we need them for a special occasion.

These files can be opened and exposed only by delving deeply into the wardrobe; they are private and personal, and not to be seen by just anybody opening a door or a drawer.

Also, we would find inside that old wardrobe our coffers, where we keep our family heirlooms and traditions of our ancestors, the culture of our countries, the legacy of several generations—religious ideals, political concepts, past memories—as a series of souvenirs separated in a box, albums of old pictures in which we find things we like to remember, personal souvenirs and portraits that we seek not to forget.

Behind these shelves we may place some journals with ups and downs, reports, and awards for great achievements, and we usually hide some old scrolls that are already outdated and even faded, but are preserved as if they were old coins that, although they cannot buy more happiness from our past, we keep because they may be worth something in the future.

We like to place on the highest shelf memories, like old jewelry, that no one could easily find or reach.

These are things we wish to stay safe and hidden, perhaps some affair to remember . . .

And then, when we least expect it, some terrible thing happens. We bump into a corner of that mental wardrobe, causing all the drawers to fall out, spilling the heavy shelves on the floor below. We try to run back to join the pieces, lamenting the fact that they are broken. We try to mend the broken parts, and a sense of guilt overtakes us. We say, "Why would I move this now? I cannot believe this is happening to me!"

Thereafter, a bed of jargon takes our words, and our attitudes of mourning can become bitter. The closet door seems to be stuck, and we soon realize that by removing things from the front and trying to reach those that were behind, we have made the clutter worse. Desperately angry, we begin to push here and there, and push harder, and we are taken by a negative reaction, asking ourselves, "Why can I not close this door? Is it possible that this thing has become jammed?"

Without stopping and asking for help, we come to a clashing temper, losing our sense of humor. We change our vocabulary and begin to utter other words, the kind that aren't in the dictionary. Anger makes us want to smash everything then and there.

Anyone who has not had that experience or something similar is very fortunate!

The Bottom Shelf: Our Subconscious

From the moment the top shelf begins to disengage the hooks of the cabinet by pulling the door and shaking the closet, the shelves begin to sag, no longer supporting their weight, becoming more cluttered and unbalanced.

We howl, scream, and try to prevent everything from falling apart, holding it on our shoulders and then falling to our knees, until finally we started screaming for help: "Please! Give me a hand over here! Oh, my goodness! Someone help me!"

Then someone comes to help, and now the scene of this drama starts to look like old dramatic scenarios played by actors masquerading in the plots of the Greek tragedies or Roman theater, in ancient dramas or modern operas of contemporary times.

Lessons from the Theater

Since mythological times, theater actors have played their dramas with masks covering their faces. In the Greek theater, actors did so out of superstition over a god's appearance in a role. The Romans followed in this theater tradition, covering their faces with masks to protect the actors and keep them from being exposed publicly for portraying their rulers in a role of criticism or a satire, making sarcastic use of imitation and mannerisms and turning their authoritarian images into jokes. This use of masks is the origin of our deployment of a persona to hide who we really are.

In the Greek theater, actors personalized their masks, using them to portray legendary tales and fantasies. Because they were all wrapped in a culture of mythological traditions, their masks represented parts of the Homeric Odyssey, where the gods are responsible for everything that is happening on the Earth's stage, with characters who act like victims or are punished because of their bad luck. Sometimes they blame it on fate, or the gods' jealousy, or spiritual guides obliging them to submissively accept a sad condition of suffering life's trials. They play out the roles that the playwright has allocated to them: crying when they have to cry, laughing when others tell the cast to laugh, yelling when they feel they are performing a specific role and cannot change. Still, they feel happy to be, so of speak, protagonists—actors and actresses who stay onstage to the end.

In this theatrical role, the dialogue and the relationships fail to be neither positive nor negative. Whether there will be a happy ending or a tragic one, the roles have to be interpreted. The other players take the same position, each one playing the role in which the dialogue was previously rehearsed, and above all, attempting to give a good performance that pleases the public. If the playwright wishes to make changes to please the critics, this will not be a problem, because the actors' role is to represent onstage what everyone wants to see.

Behind the scenes, they have to take off the makeup and costumes and get back their true image, where the real-time character becomes short and troubled by living in a cruel society, where the persona mask is replaced by a different personality on the life stage. Wearing no masks, they must still project an image of glamour, expensive living, love for the great outdoors. As actors, they still will be smiling, crying only when they're out of the limelight, where the stage lights go out. There, they hear no more the public applause. The director disappears, and what remains is the hope that one day, they can return to the stage to do another performance.

As theater developed from a simple reenactment of myths to a more sophisticated depiction of the human experience, the actors' masks became more sophisticated as well, to suit the fantasy, romance, music, songs, and melodrama—a mixture of joy, celebration, passion, selfish authority, plots, betrayal, misunderstandings, fatalities, and frustration.

The dialogue depended on who was in power. A prevailing chauvinistic figure was generally represented by an imposed authority or unyielding father figure, as in the drama of Shakespeare's *Romeo and Juliet* or Rossini's *Barber of Seville*. There follows a series of negative dialogues, arguments without interrelationships, no one willing to compromise or forgive, with no mercy and no form of reconciliation. There is betrayal, infidelity, perjury, falsehood, hatred. The stories are all about disenchantment, and they call for a terrible and lurid surrealism.

Rarely can a happy ending be found in operas. Instead, we find impossible passion frustrated by a twist of fate, where the songs are very melancholic, an opus of simultaneous dramas performed as solos, duets, and cantatas, with orchestrations and scenarios that dazzle the audience with tragic themes while being, at same time, romantic and exciting. We also see a repetition of the themes of Greek tragedies and myths, without the boredom of the gods, wherein the actors playing the roles are facing their own insatiable ego and uncontrolled passion, where people feel passion toward each other without seeking a positive relationship, just for lust and pride of the instincts, luxury of the flesh, and heated blood. They die for their love without being able to find a better way out by living for their love.

So it was with the opera *La Boheme* by Giacomo Puccini, where everything is suggested in the words of passion without thought for the most important link between two people—unconditional love. Instead, characters act in a type of naive relationship with dualistic connotations: passion or personal interest, jealousy or trust, abusive disregard or empathetic understanding, sudden decisions or constructive family plan, lovers or partners. The roles are no longer factual acts of sincere and true interpretation of shared feelings with love and friendship, respect and affection, dedication and commitment, shared understanding, and unconditioned regard. The children are determined to be joined in the same family and the parents pay the price for resisting that happy ending, realizing too late that the real reason to live is to serve, not only to be served.

The Theater of Our Lives

These theatrical themes crop up all the time in everyday life, when we make artificial appearances, exert power and control, and show our selfishness, chauvinism, superiority, dominating attitudes, individualism, and aggressive behavior. Intolerance, jealousy, envy, and many other vicissitudes are predominant in a society where most of the protagonists play an unrealistic role.

Our own dialogue with one another may be formal and fictitious, a drama of miscommunication on life's stage, where the relationships are no longer just fiction and become surreal, as a post-modern satire, and create a false feeling that this is the "real thing." As many say, "Who cares?" "Do your own thing" "Take it or leave it." See if you've read from these scripts in your own life:

Script 1:

"Hi, little woman. Are you leaving?"
"Yes, why?"
"Because I'm leaving too."
"Well, that's okay. Take it easy, old man."

Script 2:

"Yesterday, you did not tell me where you went."
"No I didn't, so what?"
"What's the matter?"
"I'm tired of telling you. Live your own life and leave me alone!"
"Right, mind your own business."

Script 3:

"I need some money, honey."
"You better slow down. You are spending too much."
"Come on, give me a break."
"No, not this time. You better control yourself, baby."
"Then you won't have sex when I get back."
"Never mind, I don't need it."
"You're getting it somewhere else, are you?"
"None of your business! Better not bug me."
"Oh yeah? Well, look here, I won't tolerate infidelity."
"That's your problem! I could not care less."
"Oh no? Well, look, I want you to leave this house!"
"Who, me? Who pays the rent, the power, and the phone?"

"You pay. But I take care of the house and our children."

"This is your domestic duty and your obligation."

"Obligation your stinking nose—you fool!"

"It is you who is to blame! You ruined my life!"

"I ruined it? I'm not the guilty one. Blame it on mommy!"

"Leave my mother out of it, you idiot!"

The curtain falls. No positive dialogue, No interrelationship.

Quite a different sort of dialogue can be found in the biblical Song of Solomon, which portrays the beauty of love as a vivid experience with a loved one. Solomon's story includes tender praises between husband and wife, who call each other "my dear" and "my love." There are no suggestions between these devoted companions to "mind your own business."

Declarations of love, affection, and appreciation not only suggest a period of courtship but offer endless romantic lines for positive relationships. The couple is always appreciative, recognizing the value of the other, respecting, caressing, and adorning, sharing their gifts and talents as something of inestimable value, with words of praise and encouragement between the two spouses. A relationship is symbolized as a charm of flowers and fragrant gardens—even with thorns in the middle of the roses, there's a sense of appreciation for the perfume that is inhaled.

Family members do not interfere in the relationship. The numerator of the events listed is implied by the difficulties faced with the same common denominator of trust, security, mutual support, and other ingredients that create the *agape* in a perfect desired interplay.

In chapters seven and eight of the Song of Solomon, we find a romantic and at the same time realistic expression of the appreciation of a true love:

The husband:

"Many waters cannot quench love, neither can the floods drown it: if a man would give all the substance of his house for love, it would utterly be contemned." (Song of Sol. 8:7).

The wife:

"I would lead thee, and bring thee into my mother's house, who would instruct me: I would cause thee to drink of spiced wine of the juice of my pomegranate." (Song of Sol., 8:2).

"I am my beloved's, and his desire is toward me. Come, my beloved, let us go forth into the field; let us lodge in the villages. Let us get up early to the vineyards; let us see if the vine flourish, whether the tender grape appear, and the pomegranates bud forth: there will I give thee my loves." (Song of Sol. 7:10-12).

Positive Words:
How to Use Them at the Right Time

The most difficult task in communication is not just knowing the words, but knowing how to manage them at the right time without losing control of the mind and the impulses of the ego, or being betrayed by the unconscious mind. Goleman's work in his treatise on the emotional coefficient is brilliant and proves that it is not enough to have the cognitive ability to use intelligence for learning and performing logically, making a decision, or solving a problem.

Even if we know how to control our emotions, it would be valuable to know how to manage a clash of words with a speaker who can be witty, indiscreet, accusatory, lying, mean, critical, cheeky, aggressive, cynical, pretentious, and terrifying, and whose purpose in most cases is not to defend himself or present his reasons or point of view but to destabilize and discredit our own arguments or bring the focus of attention to his or her personal interests, even in a bombastic, insidious or sarcastic manner.

In the media today, in times of political debates, there are experts in communication who prepare and rehearse politicians to be calm, smiling, and friendly when making their propositions in public. Above all, they are trained to avoid being caught by a plot or trick from their opponent. They are trained to answer just enough without losing their cool and composure. Instead of attacking the plans of their political adversaries, candidates must submit their own projects and concrete strategies, proclaiming their superior perspectives clearly and objectively.

When asked to give an opinion on what the opposition party did wrong or how the opponent has not yet fulfilled what he promised, a candidate will most likely say, "In my government, I will try to overcome these difficulties, with more efficient projects." Or with humility and civility, the candidate could criticize his opponent, saying, "Although I do not agree with the measures that were taken by my predecessor, I will try to pursue other priorities that will be more effective in solving this serious problem, enacting new priority measures and targeting new goals in my government."

Such a positive and nonconfrontational approach looks good in political declarations and is certainly preferable to mudslinging, but it lacks the consideration of the other person's point of view—the dialogue and thoughtful interaction in the pursuit of common denominator—that marks successful interrelationships. How do we find positive words while not locking ourselves in to an inflexible point of view? Let me be your expert communication advisor in the chapters ahead.

CHAPTER III

The Personal Relationship

In this chapter, we will discuss how a relationship can be managed and well-controlled, with both partners possessing skills to build a dialogue with positive words and an assertive manner, building mutual understanding and helping each other to succeed. The goal is a relationship that benefits both parties and achieves a common good.

We are not proposing a political strategy or some negotiation to see if anyone comes to an agreement of 50 percent or 40 percent. Indeed, a relationship should represent more than a simple contract that within a short time could wear out, and may suffer variables that modify the initial motivation and bring frustration.

During my research in South Florida for my doctoral thesis, I investigated the dynamic factors of personality in relationships and found three factors that contribute to the sort of learning process that is an essential part of successful relationships.

1. *Motivation.* A stimulus that drives our actions, motivation can be controlled, delayed, repaired, moved, and even camouflaged, depending on the factor S > R (stimulus and response of the conditioned reflex). Motivation can break out by variables that intercept the relationship between stimulus and response, arousing a conditioned reflex that can be acquired or changed by others or ourselves.

2. *Emotions.* These can come from positive or negative impulses, conscious or unconscious, even passing through a criterion of self-concept, self-analysis, self-esteem, and other psychotherapeutic constructs. An understanding of emotions will always contribute to a better understanding of personality, particularly in people victimized by trauma, inherited or acquired complex, neuroses, and maladjusted behavior. Professional supervision may provide valuable help and promote positive outcomes.

3. *Frustration.* There will always be barriers, beams, and obstacles that can undermine decisions or even prevent the achievement of a goal. But frustrations can be overcome if the individual can learn how to deal with negative conditions. These can be reversed to a positive learning process when we learn to "shake the dust and turn it up," stand up to problems, and turn wrong answers into right ones.

It is noteworthy that most of the time, people improve their social relationships in the family or at work and make considerable progress, but that has become more difficult in modern society—with family pressures, day-to-day disagreements, insecurity, unemployment, financial struggles, the demands of status in a consumer culture, inversion of values, demoralization, sophistry, debauchery, and individualistic beliefs that everyone can do whatever he wants. The media only make things worse, confusing our ethical principles and opinions based on time-honored precepts, causing us to wonder if what was right might be wrong and what was wrong might be right.

In some ways, managing a relationship is like driving a car. One must know, first, how to operate the vehicle. One must develop a feel for the road—how to speed up to pass and slow down on the corners; how to follow the curves of a hilly highway; how to stop at a red light, proceed cautiously through yellow or wait for the green; how to find a good place to park, to enter the road with caution, to change lanes. If everyone followed the rules of the road, many tickets would never be written, many accidents could be avoided, and many lives would be spared. Simple cautions could be implemented if emotions and frustrations were kept under control, and we didn't let our instincts drive us in a neurotic way, allowing anxiety to develop. A good and proper motivation to act right and make intelligent decisions will always maximize our relationships, whether with fellow motorists or with the important people in our lives.

Positive Interrelationship: Where to Start?

Collegial conversation—the friendly and social parts of a positive relationship—facilitates communication and enriches citizenship. In our day-to-day lives, we usually greet people in a cordial manner, just as a matter of courtesy. Of course, unless you're a professional diplomat, formal cordiality becomes repetitive if used constantly without any growth of familiarity. There are even courses and careers, such as human relations and public relations, that outline exactly what sort of interaction is suitable for different levels of relationship. Often, the goal is to maintain and improve good relations and facilitate interaction without ever entering into an actual positive interrelationship—the kind in which people interact with affection and mutual respect, genuine concern, and empathetic mutual appreciation, leading to agreements and enduring alliances of friendship and companionship.

Here's an example of a simple cordial relationship:

Tom: "Hi, Bob, how are you?"
Bob: "Fine, how are things going?"
Tom: "Fine."

An announcement like this one, from a public-relations department, lacks interrelationship:

"Good afternoon! We would like to inform you that we will be more than honored to receive your visit to our office. Please tell us the most convenient time and we'll be at your service."

I think we all would agree that seeking positive interrelationships with others is healthy and well-advised. Any question, perplexity, lack of clarity, misinformation, criticism, or venting—anything subjective or objective that blocks our personal search, causing terror, fear, or insecurity—points up the need for clear first steps that anyone can follow to break through the wall of anxiety and reach out to another human being.

For purposes of illustration, we will make an analogy to the principles of information science. Think of interacting with another person in the real world as you would composing and sending an e-mail. What are the steps you would take?

Step 1: Thinking Right

The man who would become the apostle Paul was once known among Christians as a religious legalistic clergyman—angry, impatient, hard with his words, a persecutor of Christians, radical, uncompromising and aggressive, a man who consented to the death of the first martyr, Stephen. Paul had a vision of the Lord Jesus when he was seeking to arrest Christians who were fleeing persecution on the road to Damascus.

From that encounter, Paul was converted to Christianity, undergoing a tremendous transformation in his character and personality, as portrayed in his letters to the churches of Asia, Macedonia, Greece, and ancient Rome. He later wrote to the Philippians: "Finally, brethren, whatsoever things are true, whatsoever things are honest, whatsoever things are just, whatsoever things are pure, whatsoever things are lovely, whatsoever things are of good report; if there be any virtue, and if there be any praise, think on these things." (Phil. 4:8).

Turning our thoughts from negative to positive—seeing the best in others and seeking things to praise rather than criticize—is a good first step in any interrelationship. Just as a hastily written and ill-considered e-mail can come back to haunt you, so can a flippant and fault-finding attitude in your interrelationships.

Step 2: Clicking Right

Once I was having problems with my computer, and I called a technician to find out what was happening. It was deleting and mixing all the commands with errors that were coming in my e-mail, and the technician found that a terrible virus had infected the memory card. I was puzzled and asked, "How did this happen? I did not send any mail to unknown sources."

The answer was simple and straightforward: "It's not what you send, but what you are receiving. All messages that arrive via the Internet, when you open them, you risk getting viruses."

"How can I avoid being infected?"

"*Just do not open the mail!*"

I learned my first lesson. On the Internet, I must examine links carefully, filter out what is negative and dangerous, and only click on what is productive and useful. Looking at trash can trash your computer. Similarly, seeking out people with whom you can only react in a negative way, whether by gossiping or arguing or sarcasm, will poison all your other interactions and relationships, bringing harm to one and all. Pass those negative opportunities over, and seek out interactions that enlighten and inspire.

Step 3: Saving Right

In the world of computing, we are aware of certain principles we must pay attention to as a matter of discipline—that is, if we are careless in these procedures, and we fail to frequently save or store useful information, we may lose valuable documents, and information of great value can be lost forever.

In relationships, what are our top priorities? What do we most seek? What would we miss the most? Here are some common things we hope for:

- Acknowledgment
- Encouragement
- Recognition
- Welcome
- Clarity
- Apology
- Forgiveness
- Approval
- Affection
- Love
- Praise
- Trust
- Support
- Instruction
- Advice

What do we need to do to preserve these functions in our relationships? We must acknowledge their value and maintain them regularly lest they fall away and are lost, taking our relationships with them.

Step 4: Addressing Right

For an e-mail message to get where it's going, the address must be correct. When we are in a hurry and have to send a message right away, we are prone to make mistakes that keep it from reaching its destination. We are often frustrated when we find that the message we mailed was returned to sender. On the Internet, proper form is crucial. Just a single letter or punctuation mark out of place can bounce the e-mail back as a wrong address.

Similarly, in an interrelationship, we must be willing to call others by the name that works for them. There are people, for example, who do not like nicknames. They do not like being called Shorty, Skinny, Fatso, Big Mouth, Four Eyes, and the like. If the name is affectionate and comes from family—such as Bobby, Little Jo, Sonny, Timmy—or comes from being popularly known as a famous player or celebrity, there is no offense. But when a nickname is used disrespectfully, there are people who prefer to be called by their birth name.

I know of two colleagues who had a great friendship until one day, one gentleman did not remember the other man's name at a wedding party. He tried to joke over it by saying, "Sorry, I do not remember your name. It was a long time ago, but I remember during our school years, they called you 'Big Nose,' right?" He didn't realize how inappropriate the name-calling was, and his (now former) friend thought he was being cocky and inconsiderate. Hard to believe someone would say such a thing, but it happened!

Sometimes when people are angry and want to retaliate in an offensive and mocking way, they'll use negative nicknames, such as "You blabbermouth!" There are people who, instead of giving a compliment, will say something they think is fun and friendly but in fact greatly offends their companion. In the middle of a party, they might joke and say, "Girl, you look chubby, did you cut your hair?" They think they have a close enough relationship to tease in this way, but quickly find out that such indiscretions only prevent future interactions.

There are also people who have a gift for encouraging others enthusiastically, saying: "Alex the great! You're doing a terrific job! I'm sorry for what happened to you, but I know you'll come out on top." Their interpersonal e-mail never bounces back.

Step 5: Sending Right

Amazingly, many times I find myself in this confusing and sometimes embarrassing situation—I make a decision to write a letter or leave a message, and then I remember the birthday has passed! Likewise, spouses may forget a wedding anniversary, or become so caught up in other activities that they fail to pick up a card or gift at the right time.

This behavior implies that the other person is not important enough for special consideration. We may feel we are honoring this person on a daily basis, recognizing his or her dignity, always being grateful for favors or hospitality received—but if the time comes to send congratulations or condolences, and we forget or come late to the date, the other person is liable to be very disappointed and hurt.

You can write a message with the best intentions, but if you do not click send and instead allow it to go to the drafts folder, it is very easy to forget to follow through and send. We cannot afford to leave the other party disappointed in this way if we want to maintain healthy interrelationships.

Step 6: Replying Right

There is no doubt that it is more difficult to respond appropriately and effectively to statements made by others than to initiate an appropriate interaction ourselves. Carl Rogers developed a client-centered counseling process in which the client must be the center of the relationship. What matters most is whether the person listening is able to respond to another's feelings in an understanding and empathetic way. Rogers calls this approach "empathic understanding" (Rogers 1961).

I remember that my students in a master's in counseling program at the University of South Alabama in 1973 needed to adjust their approach in a study of 100 patients; only 70 percent of their statements in counseling sessions brought about a good response in which the client would say, "That's right . . . that's what I mean. That's how I'm feeling."

Even more difficult was to show what Rogers called "unconditional regard" to a shocking revelation or even an absurd, compromising statement. What had to be given in response was not what the counselor thought about the situation, but concern for the circumstances the patient was in, without judging right or wrong.

This approach establishes an interrelationship between the client and the counselor. It is not recommended between therapists, but no doubt serves to improve understanding between people in which one interrelates with another unconditionally. This does not mean that the relationship between two people automatically settles down as a simple verbal interplay, but actually recognizes an empathetic understanding and expression of empathetic comprehension.

Step 7: Forwarding Right

When checking my e-mail, I can forward messages with an attachment. *Attach* means "to join, connect, bind, or dock two things together." In a relationship, it often happens that two people are walking together but not jointly—not combined from me, you, he, and she to we and they. Yet spouses, related as a family, must go together; as the Bible says: "Can two walk together, except they be agreed?" (Amos 3:3).

In a marital relationship, for the couple to have a healthy relationship, there must be an emotional rapport; the two must be interrelated in a such way that one person's enjoyment becomes the other's pleasure. This experience is also observed in a warm, emotional environment when a person is able to rejoice with the other, even cry for the other, or listen in silence to the cry of the other, appreciating the pain of the other's loss even when he or she cannot understand what in the world happened.

If, for some reason, we cannot know the situation a person is going through, it is better not to coldly say "Don't worry about it" or even "This is not the end of the world, I've been there too." This is being indifferent to another's feelings. Just knowing about a problem without an awareness of the circumstances in which the other person might be living, we fail to recognize that maybe that particular individual does not have the strength or the courage that we have. Perhaps someone is living in a different situation or facing problems in different circumstances than we have experienced before.

Finding that companionable place of mutual understanding an attachment is not easy, but it's essential. In the next chapter, we'll try to figure out a formula for making that interrelationship happen.

CHAPTER IV

The Coefficient of the Interrelationship

The coefficient of an interrelationship is the numerical indicator of a person—a sum of skills, abilities, talents, gifts, and virtues. All the qualities inherent in a human being help determine this coefficient, and it can be used to increase understanding or determine a common denominator between partners in an interrelationship.

If I'm trying to understand why a person behaves in a certain way, for example, I will look to add up a person's good points and divide that by the number of inappropriate attitudes or difficulties, taking into account a standard error that can be repaired or compensated. In statistical graphics with data, mode, and means, the average varies according to the way in which data are related in different giving patterns, creating deficiency patterns called "standard error deviations," which allow us to consider different evaluations and correct their means with proper correlation. In the same way, behavior can be evaluated, using different correlations, comparing one standard pattern with the other. Of course, every person will be different, but these are common errors that can be corrected. It should be possible to compare the differences and find a median point in which relationships can be summed up and properly evaluation by all means, together.

First Things First

Some people would say that everything is difficult at the beginning, but not always! Starting is much easier when we keep in mind the old saying, "First things first." Somehow, some way, everything has a starting point, even the quest for interrelationship.

To accomplish any task, it is important to have a realistic attitude. We must ask ourselves, how can this goal be achieved? If we want to lose weight, when should the exercise regime or dieting begin? If we want to break a record, when should we start training? If we will be taking final exams, when will we start to study? If we're going to graduate, when will we begin to design our new career? A dream brings a vision, and a vision builds a program to meet the goal.

So how, then, should someone start an interrelationship?

Step 1: Start Rehearsing

When someone learns to skate, it is impossible to begin without some falls during the first tryouts. Same with riding a bicycle—in the beginning, you need patience and persistence to learn to be on balance.

In the same manner, in our well-being projects, our goals need to be viewed with the same determination, patience, and willingness to practice and fail and practice some more. When we become competent practitioners, we will already have acquired good abilities and a valuable experience. The reason many people cannot get started in a good job is because they do not have good experience, according to the human-resources department. The requirements for filling a job can become a hindrance to many job applicants, and a lack of relationship experience can be a drawback too.

In the labor market of the modern world, when it comes to a standard of excellence or quality of service—as well as the management of human relationships in a business or work environment—candidates are assessed through tests and training to make sure they have the skills necessary for the level of relationship that will be required and will be able to form positive interactions with coworkers and employees. Usually there is a period in which trainees can experience the tensions and pressures inherent in their work environment, rehearse possible misunderstandings, resolve misinformation, and engage in problem-solving situations to determine the best solution to the problem.

Keep in mind these ten commandments for effective interrelationships:

1. *Don't* criticize other people in public. It creates antagonism and discourages others from being receptive to your communication.

2. *Don't* focus on another person's weakness without also appreciating his or her strengths—even if you can only think of a few.

3. *Don't* compare a person's abilities or personal performance to that of another who is more competent. Instead, encourage the individual to pursue realistic goals that will provide a sense of accomplishment.

4. *Don't* miss any opportunity to praise someone for achieving good results.

5. *Don't* pick on every little error. Instead, show others how to overcome their deficiencies.

6. *Don't* let your lack of control over someone be an excuse; encourage discipline whenever you can.

7. *Don't* raise your voice, even when others lose their temper. Be a model of moderation.

8. *Don't* underestimate the ability of others. Expect them to overcome their challenges.

9. *Don't* minimize self-confidence, but provide maximum opportunities to succeed.

10. *Don't* single out one person from a group; praise the teamwork.

In any game, if we grow too confident before we've actually won, we may hurry up and miss a good move, fail to foresee a checkmate, move too fast when playing checkers, or otherwise let the game slip by us before we give our best shot.

Good players need to calm down, relax, and wait for their opportunity. In sports where agility is required, like soccer, it is always necessary to take a look and determine the proper angle before kicking for the goal. In volleyball, to give a good cut, you must be cautious not to touch the net. In car racing, it's essential to know when you can overtake the lead safely, and then get into pole position.

In our "word games," the cerebellum needs to scan our memory quickly, scanning what is stored in more than a million cells and selecting the best options. Everything depends on not letting adrenaline interfere with the corticosteroids in our brains. When our emotional impulses are activated under psychological pressure—from things like insecurity, accusation, interruptions, unethical behavior, mocking, teasing, testing, carelessness, lies, blackmail, excuses, profanity, or disrespect—the best tactic would be to exercise self-control. Starting with a simple effort to be calm and slow down will help us navigate the tricky twists and turns of a testy conversation. We need to curb our impulses, take a deep breath, and have class, taking the curves carefully and then shifting to a proper gear, measuring what should be said in the right place at the right time without running off or being run over!

Example of a negative dialogue:

"Good morning!"
"Good morning, boss!"
"How are you?"
"All right. When it's possible . . ."
"Did our order come in already?"
"Not yet."
"How come? There was enough time! I've been asking for this since yesterday!"
"But that's the point—I just heard about it yesterday!"
"So you've had a whole day, you should have checked it. What's the hold-up?"
"I'm waiting for the e-mail, which did not come in."
"How did that happen? The e-mail is sent automatically!"
"Yes, but the system went down, and the computer stopped working!"
"And now, why did you not call back again?"

"I have more than one hundred people to call . . ."

"Stop calling, start checking if it came in."

"Well, how about sending money for paying the invoice? The bank is closing."

"If that is the case, our invoice order won't be confirmed!"

"It's all messed up! It's crazy around here!"

"Don't get mad! Nobody is crazy! You have to learn to do things right!"

"Then, sir, why don't you give me the right orders?"

"You better show me some more respect, man."

"Sir, you have been very rude. I did not lose any respect . . ."

"Shut up! Do not yell at me!"

Example of a positive dialogue:

"Hi, Robert!"

"Good morning, Mr. Paul!"

"How are you? Everything in order? Is there any problem?"

"Oh! Yes, the system crashed yesterday afternoon."

"It has been solved?"

"A little while ago, but we have a lot of messages coming in."

"Okay, but first check if our invoice order has arrived."

"And how about the bank? It will close in one hour."

"Let me handle that."

"Okay! No problem! You got it, boss!"

Answer these questions about the second dialogue:

- What grade would you give to this dialogue?
- What parts of the dialogue identify this as a positive relationship?
- Who used the right words?
- What are the positive words that facilitated the understanding and interconnections?
- Who assumed the leadership role, the boss or the employee?
- Who facilitated the interaction?
- What are the key words that facilitated the interaction?

Step 2: Understanding the Correlation Coefficient

All people are under a condition of being stimulated positively or negatively, and this condition will cause a conditioned reflex that is carried out physiologically or emotionally. This condition can create a constant conditioned reaction. Such reactions are observed in all living things, from a flatworm observed microscopically to wild animals, dolphins, and birds trained to perform using food rewards or such other incentives as attention, tenderness, or discipline. Punishing or rewarding a subject often provides motivation for training.

Living things obey these impulses that follow from a positive or negative response. Within applied sciences, as mathematics physics, chemistry and psychology, these factors are called variables. When two variables yield to a common denominator, one can determine a correlation between the two competing wills. According to statistical principle, two variables that move in the same direction are said to be in a positive relationship; if they move in opposite directions, their relationship is negative.

When two factors are shaped differently, they can be directed in opposite positions; however, converging in the same direction, seeking a meeting point upward, the more intense the desire to find more possibilities, the more chances of convergence for a perfect direction in the relationship.

Within a percentage scale of one to one hundred, if the correlation is around 60 percent, it is concluded that the correlation is positive and moderate. If it is below 60 percent, it is considered negative and not moderate.

If, within physical principles, we can calculate variations between two different poles to seek a decisive factor in a relationship, we can also find positive factors that make a positive interrelationships. So, if they are correlated with the determination of summing up the variables in a converging positive reaction, we can disregard those that are divergent as a negative relationship.

Cause and Effect Correlations

The correlation can be increased to the extent that the two variables compete in the same direction, up or down. This has to do with principles for converging currents, which have the ability to benefit or harm a relationship.

For example, if a vehicle's battery needs to be recharged for better performance, placing the negative cable on a negative pole and the positive cable on a positive pole will allow a current to flow through—but if we invert that, putting negative with positive, there will be a clash of cause and effect, causing a short circuit and achieving nothing.

I remember some years ago receiving a year-end honorarium, with a considerable amount to be shared with my wife. My desire was to give her half, because she had helped me with the project of digitizing and formatting work to be used in a PowerPoint presentation at my summer conferences. She thanked me kindly.

With Christmas and New Year's approaching, there was a graduation ceremony we were invited to attend, and to my surprise, she said, "Love, I am thinking of buying a new suit for you; yours is too beaten."

"Oh, dear," I replied, "do not do it. I gave you the money to buy something you might need."

Undaunted, she said, "For a long time, I have wanted to buy an Italian suit that will look great on you."

I did not know what to say when I saw her sweet smile, so I went to our room and looked at the other half of the money that I had saved and started thinking of what I could do to repay her sweet affection. I thought about a pair shoes, or perhaps a dress for the summer—all choices that were complicated, since it is not easy to choose the right style and color.

Maybe some jewelry . . . but she was very particular about that. Then I remembered that we would be traveling in the chilly season, and she had already noticed a heavy fur coat that our daughter found very elegant. Secretly, I purchased the coat on the eve of the graduation, and she purchased a suit for me.

When we were leaving home, I asked, "Are you ready for our trip?"

"Almost ready," she told me. "I've already picked out the clothes, but I'll have to borrow a coat from Elaine. My other coat is in Alabama."

So I took the box that was hidden in the closet and gave to her, smiling.

"Oh, no! You didn't spend your money on an expensive coat, did you?" she exclaimed. "We need to save money for the trip, my darling. We do not need to spend extravagantly for just one trip."

Opening the box, amazed, she said, "This is long and beautiful. I don't believe it, My heartfelt thanks, but I'm not going to use it. Please, return it. I can borrow a coat from our daughter."

To convince her, I could only say this, "My love! It's not the money or the trip, nor the coat, but what you represent to me. I accepted the Italian suit, which could be exchanged for another at a lower cost. But it was your desire and good taste to please me with the best. Now it is my turn to show my love, my affection, and my gratitude for my wife and companion, who always thinks of me first."

Selecting Words with Appreciation

There are many preconceived prejudices and opinions on what happens before and after marriage, as if it were a myth or something outdated. Some people joke about conversations between couples who date as in old times, still making loving declarations, such as *my sweet love, my sunshine, my only one, honey, sugar, my sweetheart . . .*

It is still appropriate for many couples to share their food on the same fork, stroll hand in hand, cry together when they have to be apart for traveling, write love letters, send cards, send flowers, and talk on the phone just to say *I am homesick, I missed you . . .*

"You are my love. You know that, don't you?"

Sometimes being very sincere in a trusting relationship can increase the value of the relationship.

"I must tell you one thing, but only if you promise not to get upset . . ."

"I dropped some of your plants and I broke the old vase. I am sorry, and I will buy another one."

"Look, honey, I forgot to tell you, but I promise I will make it up to you."

"I'm saying this for your good, baby . . ."

"I'm worried. Tell me, what is bothering you, honey?"

"Let us trust in God, and everything will work out."

"I admit that was difficult to handle this situation, but I'm on your side."

"I do not agree with this position, but let's think of something better."

"It was an accident, but next time I promise to warn you before . . ."

"I cannot meet you this time, but I will make that up better next time, my love."

"It was my mistake, and I sincerely apologize. I never meant for this to happen. You did not deserve this. Forgive me."

"You forgot to remember, I will fix it, the responsibility was mine."

"No matter whose fault it was, we are in the same boat. You did your part very well. Sorry, I could have helped you."

"The important thing is that we are together, and we will win this fight together!"

"I cannot do as well as you do, I understand that. But can I help?"

"Of course, looking after the children is always a great help! Sugar, you're awesome!"

In positive interrelationships, everyone wins.

Personal Inventory Test

To check the success of your own interrelationships, answer yes or no:

1. Do you accept and support the preferences of your partner?
2. Do you know how to change the subject when it is not pleasing?
3. Do you listen to an unaccepted opinion without interrupting?
4. When you argue, can you modulate the tone of your voice?
5. Do you keep yourself from getting irritated when the other person does not understand you?
6. Do you ask to better explain your point of view?
7. Do you recognize when your idea does not make sense?
8. Do you commend the person who had a better idea?
9. When you win, do you look for ways to make your partner feel better rather than crowing over the victory?
10. Do you try to calmly explain your point of view rather than yelling at your partner?

Self-evaluation: How many did you answer *yes* to?
Check your score against the evaluation below.

- *Ten*: Good answers! You have the highest interrelationship score.

- *Nine*: Your interrelationships have a great possibility of success.

- *Eight*: You have a little trouble with interrelationships.

- *Seven*: Your interrelationships still need some work.

- *Six*: Your self-concept is high but selfish.

- *Five*: You need to do a more effective job of evaluating correlations.

- *Four*: You show complacency, with little interest in others.

- *Three*: You seem indifferent to the feelings of your partner.

- *Two*: You don't know how to have a dialogue in a relationship.

- *One*: Your interactions are formal and one-sided.

If your score isn't as high as you like, don't despair—the next chapter will give you some ideas for improving it.

CHAPTER V

Ten Levels of Interrelationship

How can you increase your level of interrelationship when the correlations are low?

1. Follow the direction of the conversation.
2. Accept people as they are.
3. Avoid debate.
4. Recognize the strengths of your partner.
5. Learn from your frustration.
6. Focus on people's intentions and avoid conflicts.
7. Ask if your argument was clear.
8. Offer alternatives.
9. Listen more than you speak, and speak only as needed.
10. Learn to be a facilitator.

We'll look at many of these in more detail in this chapter, while holding two back for chapters of their own.

Follow the Direction of the Conversation

Participating in a conversation without taking sides is an art. The most important issue is to moderate the dialogue to maintain a posture of seeking solutions of interest to your partner, family, children, group, council, board, circle of friends, social group, community organization. There will always be a reason to find a good strategy that leads to common grounds.

Assuming leadership means taking the reins to prevent the carriage from overturning with you inside, taking the helm so that the boat will not capsize, taking the lead with people who are part of the conversation. It also requires you to recognize that although you will contribute to achieving the goal, the win belongs to the team.

It's not worth it to swim against the tide. Good fishermen learn early to get onboard with the rudder to the beach. You reach the other side faster.

Consider this dialogue as it demonstrates the dynamics of group relationships:

"By order, Mr. President!"

"Yes, what is the order?"

"You did not put my request on the agenda."

"The agenda has been approved already."

"But my proposal was not placed on it."

"What was your subject?"

"The budget report for the new construction!"

"This report has been read and approved without amendment."

"How it was approved? It was not voted on!"

"It was voted on in the previous session."

"Why was I not told about it?"

"It was noted, it was because you were not present during our discussion . . . The question you have raised is out of order, but in consideration to your request, I will forward the report approved by this floor for your review, as soon this session is completed."

This dialogue was based parliamentary procedure, in which questions are answered in such a way as to head off criticisms, divergent views, thematic disagreements, arguments, objections, and outbursts. There are rules and priorities established by corporate bylaws, but the president spoke with good manners and in a way that was appropriate to the relationship. He considered the other person's view with unconditional regard, even when ruling that the question was out of order.

Accept People as They Are

I remember a time when I was invited to perform the marriage ceremony of a well-known family in town. At the crowded wedding reception, it was impossible to meet and greet everyone. We looked forward to chatting with the family of the bride and groom and other guests. By coincidence, the city mayor greeted us and commented on the message I delivered at the wedding ceremony. As we were leaving, a couple came to greet us, saying, "How are you, Dr. Ivan? You no longer speak with the poor?" Pointedly, the wife said, "You now only have time for high-class people?"

Smiling and putting my hands on their shoulders, I replied, "On the contrary, I would like to talk to the poor in spirit too, because Jesus said: 'Blessed are the poor in the spirit, for theirs is the kingdom of heaven.'"

And then with a kind of wondering, they asked, "Does that mean that a person has to be poor in the spirit to enter heaven?"

"What did Jesus imply?" I responded. "The materially poor, so to speak? The ones who are poor of intellect? The poor of high living and social recognition? I think He meant those who are not materially rich, thinking of others instead of themselves, humble ones, living with simplicity, considering others more important."

"Bless you, pastor, you just made a point. We got the message."

During this situation, if I had tried to apologize for not noticing the couple, or had chosen a way out by saying that I had been greeted by the mayor, I would still be giving an impression of inflating my position. Instead, I turned the technique of effective acceptance to the question of accepting people the way they are. We should always be willing to extend our hand to reach others at the level where they are socially, financially, intellectually, emotionally, and spiritually.

Avoid Debate

Whenever a political candidate is challenged by his opponent to a debate, analysts always say that preparation is needed to know how to let things go without resorting to antagonistic attacks that can compromise the candidate's image or counter his arguments.

At the end of a debate, the media seeks to declare a winner or determine who had a greater impact on the voting public. Not everything should be discussed, though, because what matters are not issues that magnify the weaknesses of the candidate, but their strategies for solving problems and their proposed solutions for achieving goals.

An example of how to avoid confrontations that bring conflict occurred during the campaign for the presidency of the United States by incumbent Jimmy Carter and challenger Ronald Reagan. Reagan was constantly challenged by his opponent with the same questions from previous debates that had already been answered.

Reagan was advised not to get carried away by the insidious way in which President Carter kept challenging his positions on Medicare and Social

Security, but with a smile and good humor, Reagan replied, "There you go again." Everyone laughed, and the issue was defused.

Debate should be used to clarify facts, not to throw mud or raise unwarranted accusations or presumptions. Questions about morality, dishonesty, and intimacy should be addressed by a competent authority and with the right of defense.

Recognize the Strengths of Your Partner

I used to teach my students, when I was giving lectures about leadership, that one of the biggest weaknesses of a strategist is to fail to recognize the strengths of his competitor. When I refer to this position, I'm not just saying, "We should not underestimate our opponents." Instead, I'm suggesting that people who are opposed to our ideas or disagree with our views are not our enemies. They simply have different or divergent beliefs from ours, and often they have strong principles based on their own philosophies, religious concepts, and traditions.

Back in the 1940s, it was said that, rather than try to convince a Communist that he was wrong, it was better to argue that there were better ideas within socialism. This approach was less alienating and more constructive, giving the individual a real issue to think about.

Our tendency is to stand by our convictions, our reasons, our guesses. But when a person says, "I believe this, so I will not change my mind," it is better to change the subject or clearly demonstrate that we respect his point of view.

When an interrelationship needs to be established, a more consistent point is to simply say that we respect others with their ideas, and we want to learn about them. This ethical position implies that in addition to respecting the other person, you recognize that the individual is potentially informed on the subject or has a solid background in the issues being raised. The other person, in turn, will have a chance to enjoy or appreciate your point of view, building into this interaction a positive correlation rather than a negative one. Convergences always lead to a contemplation of various angles of an appreciation of what would be the best alternative, so that both can walk together.

Once I observed a very complicated debate in BoaTerra ("The Good Land"), State of Bahia, northeastern Brazil, in an education forum on

Afro-Brazilian Culture during a high-school teacher's seminar. At first, I considered adding the controversial topic of cults and African culture as well, supported by African descendents in that region, implying that the religious culture of Brazil was rooted in beliefs in their saints and gods and the offering of animal sacrifices, a basic creed of Animalism. The issue was whether the high-school students should study these subjects as part of their academic programs in their public schools.

A professor of general history began her argument by implying that because Brazil was a country whose contribution was indeed Afro-cultural, influenced by historical and cultural tradition and ancient religions practiced by their African ancestors, this subject should be included in high-school classes as part of the curriculum of the State Board School Program, which included arts, folklore, and religious background. This professor noted that the great part of the black race and culture in Brazil came from Africa during slavery times.

Another teacher readily endorsed and acknowledged this argument, trying to justify the views put forth by the speaker to the school board.

A Christian leader cleverly asked if it would be in order to consider some points of divergence from that proposition. and he was given the floor.

The Christian leader began, "Is it fair that we admire your African culture as a historical and cultural legacy? Yes! I think so, it is more than fair. However, we need to recognize Africa as a continent and not as just a nation, because this case about African culture is a different issue that has been inserted in this context. We should take into consideration the fact that among other nations in the large African continent, there are countries of different religions, such as Egypt, South Africa, Somalia, Sudan, Ethiopia, Nigeria, Morocco, Cameroon, Zaire, Libya, and Tunisia; and people of other faiths who do not profess Candomblé, Macumba, or Voodoo, but have different beliefs such as Catholicism, Buddhism, Islam, Hinduism, Protestantism, and other religious segments totally differentiated by their creed and faith, who also immigrated to Brazil with their religious beliefs as part of the Afro-religious culture of our country of multiple creeds and beliefs."

After this clarification, all agreed that the list of disciplines should be revised and could be studied in a course on comparative religion once and for all, to accommodate the religious beliefs of various African traditions as a whole and not as a part. And conclusively, a strong point was established and recognized by both sides.

Focusing on People's Intentions and Avoid Conflicts

What would be the best way for an interrelationship to be productive and avoid conflicts? To this end, it is necessary to focus on the objective of the question at the beginning of an interrelationship. We can always find someone who is angry because something happened unexpectedly—conflicts with business, with family, with traffic, a misunderstanding with neighbors, partners, children, teens, mother, daughters, the landlord . . . Daily, we are subjected to setbacks and disappointments that, if not resolved satisfactorily, will be discharged directly or indirectly as a time bomb for someone.

Other types of internal conflicts that are not healed or have never received adequate therapeutic treatment may have been stored in our subconscious, as in cases of repressed trauma that is never properly resolved. There are others, deeper traumas that come from ages past, which may have generated different types of neuroses and therefore need professional care by competent therapists.

Focusing on the reaction rather than the intent can make these time bombs go off and drive away any possibility of interrelationship. Control yourself and your emotions when others cannot, and you may be able to avoid conflict and leave the door to positive interaction open.

Ask If Your Argument Was Clear

There is another major barrier to establishing an interrelationship that occurs at the beginning of a conversation or dialogue. Generally, we start talking about something and move to a different topic, and then someone makes another statement and it looks like we are agreeing, and later we want to clarify that this was not what we were talking about, and someone will say, "You said, yes! Now you want to change sides."

Please do not let this get complicated. This makes a relationship into a mere exchange of speeches in which two or more people will discuss most of the time what was said by whom and what was unsaid. An interrelationship, to be positive, must establish two points of view; even though these may differ, they must converge to the same theme, which sets the two sides of the issues being discussed by stakeholders, each having an understanding of the point of view of the other. In this way, we can find what we call the "approach to the issue."

Asking the person if your argument was clear does not mean that the other person agrees, just that he clearly understands your position and what the basis of your argument is. Most of the time, people talk a lot, get excited, and do not pay attention to what is being said.

Take, for example, this conversation between two colleagues at the same university.

"Look, buddy, we have some possibility of expanding our postgraduate courses, as there is a great demand for journalism and tourism."

"Great, but look, we cannot suggest any possibility without consulting the Department of Higher Education, right?"

"Yes, of course . . . and what do you think of expanding our journalism offerings?"

"It is worthwhile to study this possibility, but again, it is useless to do anything without prior consultation with the Secretary of the Department of Education."

"Okay, but let me turn back to my first statement. As I said, I did a survey of the possibility of expanding postgraduate courses, that's all."

"I get it, but no use wasting time without consulting . . ."

"Excuse me, but it seems that my dear colleague has not understood my point."

"Of course I did! I just do not want to waste time on a project without consultation!"

"Well, answer me this: The first phase of our research is to design the new courses to be sent to the Secretary. We have to study the demands of the public target, the basis of the course, costs, hiring new teachers, the availability of classrooms, the number of vacancies to be offered, and other important things."

"Yes, it's clear that this is the initial phase of the draft . . ."

"I am so sorry, mate, but that's what I've been telling you from the beginning of our conversation. The important point is that our survey is in the initial phase, and this is our first draft."

"Oh! Well, now this is very clear, but we cannot do anything without consulting . . ."

"Oh my goodness! Here we go again . . ."

"Without consulting *the secretariat*!"

What is the point of this dialogue? I was trying to clarify two points of view, which turned to different angles, but engaged in a common purpose of expanding the college program with new courses. In this case, one person was arguing the need to proceed with a survey, while the other properly observed that there were common procedures and standards of institutional practice that caused her concern. The plan was facing a bureaucratic step that prevented one speaker from understanding the purpose of a survey for two new courses, which were within the institution's plan goals and ready to be approved by the Department of Education with all its previous requirements.

Listen More Than You Speak, and Speak Only When Needed

This principle is one of the most popular techniques in counseling, psychotherapy, and psychoanalysis. It requires training, posture, and personal control. Awareness is important for understanding the inquirer who needs help to demonstrate what he thinks, and for picking up on nonverbal communication you might miss while you're talking.

The meaning and interpretation of words are like a confirmation of what one is trying to express. Words like *What? How? Why? For what?* are inserted into a conversation, and the listener's understanding of the speaker's situation brings meaning to these expressions. The following are examples of key sentences that, with some warmth of inflection and positive understanding—that is, empathetic and unconditional regard—facilitate an opening for a positive interrelationship.

- "How are you feeling?" (Not as empathetic)

- "How was your day today?"
  (More comprehensive)

- "What is happening?" (More investigative)

- "Want to talk about something that is bothering you?" (Supportive)

- "Feel free to talk, whatever you want talk about . . ." (Relaxing)

These phrases establish a positive interrelationship, establishing a higher correlation and higher coefficient in order to facilitate an empathetic understanding. Consider these exchanges between client (C) and therapist (T), and how they demonstrate different types of interaction.

C: "No one understands my situation."
T: "You feel like you are alone in the crowd." (Interpreting)

C: "I cannot take it anymore."
T: "It makes you want to drop everything, right?"

C: "Nobody understands my situation . . ."
T: "As in, no one is listening to you, right?" (Empathic Understanding)

C: "I do not know who else to call."
T: "You feel like you are at a dead end . . ." (Deep Empathy)

C: "I know that I made terrible mistake!"
T: "Nobody is perfect . . ." (Unconditional Regard)

C: "I did not listen to my parents . . ."
T: "You feel guilty about that . . ." (Support)

C: "I'm tired of fighting."
T: "It has been going over your limits . . ." (Leading)

C: "This makes me want to cry! I'm sorry . . ."
T: "Take your time, you can open up, I'm listening to you." (Assuring Trust)

C: "I do not believe in anyone else!"
T: "Sometimes it is difficult to trust in someone . . ."
  (Reaffirming)

C: "I think I need to find a way out, I cannot go on
  with it any longer."
T: "You need a big break to lay off all this things . . ."
  (Driving)

C: "I do not know how to stop, to start, or how to
  go by . . ."
T: "I am here to help to find where to start it over . . ."
  (Submitting the Relationship)

C: "This is bothering me. I want forget my failures
  more than anything . . ."
T: "Something has been bothering you . . ."
  (Facilitating Catharsis)

C: "I want to know how handle this."
T: "Let's find a way to handle this and to hold on
  to . . . ?" (Secondary Reinforcement)

C: "I am very sad that happened to me . . ."
T: "This makes you suffer very much?" (Empathic
  Understanding)

C: "Sometimes I am very angry."

T: "Many times we have to feel angry about bad things." (Unconditional Regard)

The second task is to try to empathize and be able to demonstrate that we stand in their shoes, implying that we realize what the person is experiencing. A second group of phrases are useful now that we are talking, when we have established a rapport and a positive interrelationship:

- "I can imagine that it is not easy to face this situation."
- "It's like standing in a blind alley."
- "There are no words to describe the loss of a son."
- "This must have left you mad with rage."
- "It was as if a hole in the ground was opened under your feet."
- "Your unemployment situation can bring great disappointments."
- "Being a working wife and mother with an unemployed husband is like a nightmare."
- "I feel that this is a heavy burden to you, as a widow to support five children . . ."

All these statements should not be stereotyped, as mere repetition; above all, they should be used to express empathetic understanding—that is, to demonstrate that you understand the situation so that the other person perceives that and feels supported by the way he or she can express the words back to you.

Moreover, these phrases reflect a sincere position, without bias or influence of our own point of view; we aim to understand the circumstances the person is or was in so we can help. This type of approach is for strengthening the interrelationship to an understanding, unconditional regard—to facilitate the relationship, break down barriers, reaffirm mutual trust, and demonstrate that there is a deep interest in helping and supporting and correlating with each other in a narrower and more meaningful way of trust.

CHAPTER VI

Learning from Our Frustrations

There is an old American saying: "Only two things are inevitable—death and taxes." Although it sounds like a joke, it is very true. So true that we must admit that everyday life is not just a matter of winning and losing, to keep us from being frustrated. Everything we do, or don't do, will affect us directly or indirectly. It's a *sine qua non* condition, an indispensible condition that needs to come into focus.

In this section, we propose to examine how we deal with frustration. Generally, when we bump into other people, we need to adjust the level of our expectation, because the higher our expectation, the greater will be our frustration.

We tend to label ourselves as victims of mistakes or failures, and are often disappointed when others take a different attitude. We are disappointed and say things to ourselves like:

"Why did I trust them?"

"It's always like this, we try to help them, and we end up getting hurt . . ."

"I knew it; I knew it was going down the drain with this guy."

Dealing with frustrations and learning how to avoid them is the most effective way to ensure that a relationship will endure without great disappointment.

Here are some theories to be considered on frustrations.

The Reflex Theory of Ivan Pavlov

In Pavlov's experimental tests, it was proven that one can control the behavior of a dog when the stimulus (S) requires a response (R). After several attempts, the unconditioned reflex may become conditioned.

Pavlov rang a bell every time he called his dog to give him food. Then, he observed that even without giving food, when the bell rang, the dog salivated, anticipating food.

Behavioral Theories of B.F. Skinner

While at Harvard, B.F. Skinner invented the operant conditioning chamber, popularly referred to as the Skinner box, to measure responses of organisms (most often, rats and pigeons) and their orderly interactions with the environment. Skinner discovered that consequences for the organism played a large role in how the organism responded in certain situations. For instance, when the rat would pull the lever, it would receive food. Subsequently, the rat made frequent pulls on the lever.

Every time the stimulus brought satisfaction and pleasure without learning, the organism was only stimulated by pleasure. There was only the motivational relationship of pleasure and satisfaction. This was called *primary reinforcement.*

When the stimulus was a barrier (variable) that prevented a prompt response, with difficulties to be overcome, the reflex become conditioned, as the organism learned to extract a positive experience that would be rewarded every time. This was called *secondary reinforcement.*

Operating Conditions

When conditions are favorable and the attempt continues with persistence, there is compensation and the working condition is positive—that is, it contributes to constructive learning. If, on the other hand, the condition is bad and needs to be worked out, alternative solutions must be sought until the condition is reversed to a positive bias and reward.

If these rules are true in determining the behavior of beings inferior to man, much more could be expected of human beings. Despite a universe of complexities inherited, acquired, and generated, humans have immeasurable potential alternatives, with amazing ability to adapt with extrasensory flexibility, decisiveness, quick thinking, and cognitive intelligence superior to other beings, and with consciousness to review the past, understand the present, and plan for the future. This makes a huge difference in a holistic approach toward the perfect gifts of body, soul, and spirited human beings.

Based on this dynamic factor of personality development, theorists Alfred Adler and John B. Watson began to study human behavior and relationships based on knowledge acquired by motivations, emotions, and frustrations in the interrelationship.

Other behaviorists say categorically that only human beings can learn in a dynamic way how to deal with frustrations and be able to adjust to situations on more favorable terms than other inferior beings, which has presented the lowest cognitive level in self-learning as a didactical way in which teaching methods can be learned. The human has a stronger will and determination to overcome difficulties or obstacles.

As humans, we can make our own decisions even when we are under pressure, making the right choices without being manipulated, except in case of survival. There is evidence that, regardless of ethnicity, environment, social class, or educational level, anyone can opt for a new trial; even when it is tough and difficult to overcome and you have to fight to get the frustrations out, you learn that for every little door that closes there is a hope and a new experience to be attempted and new doors to open.

It is said that Thomas Edison, the inventor of the lightbulb, became frustrated fifty-one times with his experiment and started all over again, with patience and hope that he could create a little filament on an electric current to radiate a beam of light. Each frustration caused the scientist to continue more tenaciously, until, on the fifty-second try, he successfully made it!

Example of a Counseling Session, Dealing with a Frustrated Life

I was once called on to advise the state school board about a situation of a Chinese mother who was dealing with a very dramatic problem. Her husband was a hopeless alcoholic. He would come home very late and brutally beat the poor woman in front of their children. The school board asked me to develop a case study of the situation.

I asked the women if she would like police protection. She sadly told me, "If my husband is arrested, they will deport him, and my children cannot study here and stay here by themselves anymore. And I would have to go back to my Communist country, and it will be much worse."

One day, she came smiling into my counseling office, telling me, "The problem is over!"

I thought that her husband had disappeared or died, but she explained, "When he was beating me, I made a prayer, asking God to have pity on him and help him with his sadness and frustration. He stopped beating me and soon he started hugging me, apologizing and saying that this was the last time I would see him drunk! He returned to work the next morning and became a good husband and father to our family, just like he was before when we lived in China."

It sounds like a miraculous story, and perhaps it may have been, but the point of the matter was that, even under the frustration of literally being beaten, in a painful and offended posture, this woman was decisive in showing that she felt pity for her husband, demonstrating that the old interrelationship could be restored. The persistence to wait for the right time to demonstrate that she loved her family, even if it was necessary to pay a high price, was worth the rescue.

An Example of a Transference Process:
A Frustrating Experience Transformed to a Better Attitude.

A nurse's husband was always complaining that his wife had to work late hours and weekends at the hospital. Sometimes if she was home on Saturday, she could not ask to be off on Sunday.

They always ended up fighting, because the husband claimed not to have a proper marital life because the wife was always tired. His frustration was aggravated by the fact that his salary was insufficient to support his entire household. His wife had to supplement the family income by working difficult night shifts.

Instead of recognizing that his companion was trying to help the household by working, he would complain at home in front of his three children, saying, "If it were up to me, she would never work." One day he insulted her, screaming, "You think because you work, you don't have to satisfy me? You are very wrong! You have to give me more attention!"

The wife, unable to endure the abuse any longer, said, "Okay, I'll stop working. I will take care of the house, you, and the children!"

He thought she was venting and stopped insulting her. The next morning, when she did not leave for work, the following dialogue took place:

"What is this about? Are you off today? What happened?"
"I had enough yesterday from all your insults! My work is now at home!"
"But my dear, how about the expenses, who will pay?"
"Just like you said: the woman's place is at home!"
"Yes, but my salary just does not cover all the household expenses."
"Sell your car, and go to work by bus!"
"But the car is greatly needed . . ."
"But your wife must do much more for her family than anything else!"
"Wait a minute, let's talk . . ."
"Well, let's clear this up. The point is that you've been frustrated being a taxi driver while I have been a nurse. I have known that for a long time. Now, let me say one thing. This is no cause for shame. It makes no difference if I go to work

or if you earn more, or who spends more time at home. The important thing is to admit that the two of us have work, and no one has to take the blame for the other. I'm not going take this anymore. We have to face reality!"

"All right, my angel, you're right. I've been a fool. Forgive me!"

"What is most important in all this, my husband, is that we are paying private school tuition for our children to have a better education and a better future."

"It's true! From now on, I'll put my frustration aside. Whenever I cannot have you at home, I will remember that we are working hard for a great reward: the future of children, the welfare of the family!"

This mismatch of frustration needed to be checked by the operating conditions. It seemed at first to be a negative condition; however, since secondary reinforcement was used by the wife who saw her husband only taking into account the primary reinforcements to meet their wishes, without learning positive values.

The "Corns" of Our Lives

Often, we meet people who literally have a callus on their foot. They're always protecting it so that no one can touch, bump, or worse, step on it! They focus on not getting hurt.

When I was a kid, my father, as a good northern Brazilian, had a callus on his left big toe. One morning he was stretching his legs on a big chair, trying to rest after lunch. He always used to warn me, "I'll take a nap, please do not stumble on my toes."

One day, I stumbled upon the balcony running through the doorway and stepped on his toes. He woke up screaming, yelling at me, "What the heck is going on! Can I not rest and take a nap? Why don't you try to do something in your room?"

Being a good-hearted person, my father rarely gave me an earful. He could tolerate most things, unless someone stepped on his toes.

That was true not only literally, but also rhetorically. In his relationships with others, if anyone touched on certain of his personal views, it would be like touching his weak spot. In Greek literature, it is called the Achilles heel. It was *ouch, ouch, ouch*! He could lose his temper easily and become very aggressive, to the point where some people would ask, "What has gotten into him?"

My mother, who came from a German background, simply said, "Don't worry about it. You just stepped on his toes. It is going to be all right."

What was the corn of my old father? If someone tried to put something over on him or outsmart him, he would say, "Are you thinking I'm a stupid redneck? If you want, I can help you of my own free will, but if you are trying to cajole me, to win something from me, and to fool me, then I'll be mad at you."

There are calluses that are marked by frustrations from the past, and there are other traumas that have wounded the soul of the people and been repressed in the subconscious—modifying their personality, making relationships bitter, and sometimes making them aggressive to the point of being intolerable.

In your interrelationships, be sensitive to these sore spots in your partner, and try not to let your own frustrations grow to such a point that they must not be stepped on. Corns only get in the way of a true sharing of emotions, goals, and viewpoints.

CHAPTER VII

Learning to Be a Facilitator

From time to time, we all may feel the need to improve our interrelationship with someone—a husband, wife, son, daughter, father, mother, brother, sister, father, mother, partner; a colleague at work, in sport, the community, the fraternity, the congregation; your staff, membership, or ministers associated with a component of their choir, the department of education, or discipleship. These types of relationships may be formal, or simple; they may involve leadership, professional communication, or personal matters. Conversations can become collegial, but when you need them to go deeper, to establish a relationship in a more enriching way, you need to use approaches that facilitate communication and, thereby, a more effective interrelationship.

An Example of Misused Leadership

Once, I attended a leadership seminar on discipleship in which the leader intended to help his audience better understand temperament, personality, leadership skills, quality of work performance, dedication, and submission to the fulfillment of this mission of guidance. The leader conducted this seminar under a strict discipline and even made assessments of the team members' own training. I realized, while chatting during a coffee break, that a minister of a church in Canada was not very enthusiastic and remained silent and reserved, not attending a demonstration of the group repeating the words of the seminar leader, who was asking over and over to get response by his vibrating voice:

"How do you like our seminar?"

"Wonderful! Wonderful! Wonderful!" all responded.

I thought for a moment that perhaps Canadians were more reserved when it came to externalizing feelings, and perhaps this was a group of colleagues who were not well-matched with each other, outside their enthusiasm.

But then I realized the ovation and the applause were not manifested collectively. When I got closer to a participant, I ventured to ask, "How do you like this seminar?"

He replied, "The seminar is good, but the leaders are very tough."

Looking facilitate the communication, I emphasized his words: "Very tough?"

Then he continued, "Well, when I came down to the hall for the coffee break, I crossed the hall to get me a Coke, but one of the leaders rushed over to me and told me, 'You are not allowed to go to the hotel lobby, you have to eat only in our meeting room.'"

I said, "You got a kind of bad feeling with this embarrassing situation . . ."

And he answered, "Yes, because I asked if it was a hotel rule, or from the seminary's staff? He said, 'It is our staff's decision!' And then he just left."

I continued the interaction about his personal views on the training, and then I realized that the way it was conducted was inappropriate. Wrong approaches were made, without affection, in which the problem was not with the content and discipline that was required for a course of discipleship, but the hard impositions placed on the setting.

In an intensive training regimen, whether military or civilian, it is considered normal that the conditions created to promote meaningful interrelationships should be open and clear, to be well-understood by both parties within the content of their rules and acceptable discipline.

An example is receiving superior orders in the military services in a show of tough discipline. "Marine!" the top sergeant screams as he gives the orders, and the subordinate also shouts and says, "Yes, sir!" He understands the discipline in this setting will be strict, and he know how they will both respond. In sports, the coach usually yells at his players, but it is clear that they know the rules of the game, and they are participating in the training with consent of both parties, with mutual understanding.

At the training seminar, there was no such understanding, and no effort by the leader to set clear expectations. So the discipline delivered seemed arbitrary and detracted from the effectiveness of the program. The leaders clearly did not have empathy for the participants, and were motivated only by their feelings of power and importance.

Empathetic Understanding in a Family Relationship

Consider this discussion between spouses experiencing complications in planning a family getaway.

"Honey, don't be offended, you know that I do not like doing things in a hurry, but we do not have another flight for tomorrow, only late hours."

"But the point is that you made reservations at the last minute."

"I acknowledge that, but did not know whether the strike would continue in the notary office."

"I prefer to wait till next week and calmly prepare for this long trip."

"According to the list, reservations will only be three weeks from now."

"Yes, dear, I need to buy a few items of warm clothing and stock up on my medicine."

"What if I helped you by going out to buy these things this afternoon?"

"You need to pass by my doctor's office to get the prescriptions and fill them at the pharmacy. Can you do all that in time?"

"I can. You call me later, and I'll come back to pick you up."

"Don't know if I will make it on time, the shopping center will be closed."

"The mall closes at ten p.m."

"And your meeting is scheduled for eight p.m., isn't it, honey?"

"The agenda is easy, and I will ask the vice president to take it over."

"Can we make this trip in time for Christmas, even with so many things to do? We have to wake up tomorrow at four a.m. for the six-thirty flight."

"Okay, I agree to postpone for the coming month."

"I do not want to undo your plans, love . . . but the time to do things is very tight."

"I guess the point is, we need to fulfill all our plans, so why not wait."

"What's making you hurry?"

"Because I like to spend the New Year with our children and grandchildren."

"I get it now, honey. It makes a big difference to get there before the holidays, when everyone is gathered together as a large family celebration."

"I think we can agree on this very important point for the whole family. Come on, let's hurry!"

"Great, my dear, you were right, you have agreed to pay the price and wear yourself out, but I promise that I will repay you. Give me a kiss, sweetheart."

"Come on, my darling, help me pack the suitcases. We have little time, but we will succeed!"

What did you think of this conversation?

- Utopian?
- Idealistic?
- Plausible?
- Realistic?
- Practiced?
- Weighted?
- Applicable?
- Reachable?
- Altruistic?
- Beneficent?

The fact is that everything was said with good manners and with meaningful affection, even with all the pressures, showing that an ideal relationship can be accomplished. It also could be compared to a musical duet, following the same music harmonically. Using a score, although one is the soprano and the other the bass, the notes can be reconciled, and together they sing a beautiful melody that delights, dazzles, and restores each to the other, inspiring and making them sing with their souls, rejoicing in their spirits, bringing peace.

CONCLUSION

To summarize, I believe that relational intelligence has quietly asserted itself into the lives of multitudes around the globe today, and has taken its place as a guide to the uplands of intelligent life for the late twentieth century.

Everywhere I have traveled, I have met those whose lives have been changed by countless new methods of modern world communication, adding thousands of words to our vocabulary and an ocean of different expressions, and it seems that we have been unaware of their tremendous impact over the past fifty years.

I hope you have found some good tools to create what you need to achieve an effective interrelationship, and to be a good predictor of future behavior, using your intelligence by immersing yourself in all that resides in your core of your consciousness.

I believe it is part of God's plan for this world that we should love one another, using not only knowledge but, above all, our wisdom as a gift from God.

Whatever you have learned in this process of human relationship, live it with passion, energy, and in good faith, with undaunted spirit that will light a fire within you, in a way that others will be enlightened by you.

And remember, "Every good gift and every perfect gift is from above, and cometh down from the Father of lights, with whom is no variableness, neither shadow of turning. Of his own will begat he us with the word of truth, that we should be a kind of first fruits of his creatures." (James 1:17-18)

Ivan Pitzer de Souza

ABOUT THE AUTHOR

What led the author of this book to introduce different aspects of interpersonal relationship was the *raison d'être* of all interpersonal or intrapersonal relationships—relational intelligence, both intellectual and emotional, that carries an assumption, undergoes a process of stimulus and response, and leads the subject to relate in a positive or negative way with an understanding of himself or others as far as family relationships, the environment, and work, whether in the fields of commercial, political, education, health, or religion, within a degree of intelligence, determining a person be successful or unsuccessful.

ABOUT THE BOOK

The focus of this book is on the question of interrelationship as our duty, as suggested by the word *reciprocity*, defined as "helping one another."

Our mission is essential and founded on love and compassion within unrestricted human solidarity. We have encouraged many who needed to understand their roles within the dynamics of their personalities and the framework of personal interrelationships.

The author goes beyond the superficial traits of a relationship to a closer assessment, evaluating motivations and frustrations as dynamic factors that begin with what a person wants to achieve for herself and moves on to what can be expected from others in her circles of friendship.

From our Master, we have learned the most important maxim of Christianity: "Love your God above all things, and your neighbor as yourself." Although it is a difficult mission, we must learn from Him that our solicitude will be a direct reasonable approach for a reciprocal kind of love.

REFERENCES

Charcot, JM. 1885. *Leçons sur du Maledies Nerveux System, Sapêtrière*. Paris.

Gardner, Howard. 1983. *Frames of Mind: The Theory of Multiple Intelligences*. New York: Basic Books, Harper Collins Publisher, Inc.

Goleman, Daniel. 1996. *Emotional Intelligence*. New York: Bloomsbury Publishing.

Rogers, Carl. 1961. On Becoming a Person: A Therapist's View of Psychotherapy. New York: Houghton Mifflin.